Judges 11-21

"Life Without God"

A Bible-Based Study
For Individuals and Groups
Complete with Leader's Guide

Lamplighters International
Eden Prairie, Minnesota, USA 55344
www.LamplightersUSA.org

Third printing – October 2003

Lamplighters International
Eden Prairie, Minnesota USA 55344

© 1996 by Lamplighters International. All rights reserved worldwide. International copyright secured.

No part of this book may be reproduced in any form without written permission from the author and Lamplighters International except for brief quotations for review purposes.

Scripture taken from the New King James Version. Copyright © 1982 by Thomas Nelson, Inc. Used by permission. All rights reserved.

Lamplighters International is a Christian ministry that publishes Bible-based, Christ-centered discipleship materials and other resources.

For additional information about the Lamplighters ministry resources contact:
Lamplighters International P. O. Box 44725, Eden Prairie, Minnesota USA 55344 or visit our web site at www.LamplightersUSA.org.

ISBN # 1-931372-05-5

Order # Ju2-NK-SS

Contents

How To Use This Manual   4

1a/b Pride And Prejudice   7
      Ju. 11:1-12:15

2a/b The Double-Minded Deliverer   13
      Ju. 13:1-16:31

3a/b The Fruit Of Self-Deception   19
      Ju. 17:1-18:31

4a/b The Depth Of Depravity   25
      Ju. 19:1-20:48

5a/b Right In Their Own Eyes   31
      Ju. 21:1-25

Leader's Guide   37

How To Use This Manual

What is Lamplighters?

Lamplighters is a Christ-centered ministry that is designed to increase your understanding of God's Word and equip you to serve Him more effectively. The ministry consists of student and teacher curricula, discipleship Bible studies and leadership training materials.

This Lamplighters Bible study can be completed individually as a self-study Bible study guide, as a study guide for group Bible study or as a student workbook for an adult Bible class. Each lesson within this study is a self-contained unit and is an integral part of the entire Lamplighters discipleship ministry.

This Lamplighters study is comprised of five or ten individual lessons depending which format you use. When you have completed the entire study you will have a much greater understanding of a significant portion of God's Word. You will also have learned several new truths that you can apply to your life.

How to study a Lamplighters lesson.

A Lamplighters study begins with prayer, your Bible, the weekly lesson, and a sincere desire to learn more about God's Word. The questions are presented in a progressive sequence as you work through the study material. You should not use biblical commentaries and other biblical reference books until you have completed your weekly lesson and met with your weekly group. When you approach the Bible study in this way, you will have the opportunity to discover valuable personal insights from the Word of God.

First, find a quiet place to complete your weekly lesson. You will need approximately thirty minutes to complete each lesson (Part "A" or Part "B"). If you are new to Lamplighters, plan to spend more time on the first few lessons. Your weekly personal study time will decrease as you become familiar with the format. Soon you will look forward to discovering important life principles in the coming lessons.

Some people complete their weekly lesson at one time but others have found it beneficial to complete the studies on two different occasions. If you approach your study time in this way you will be able to reflect more fully upon difficult biblical passages. For those meeting as part of a study group or an adult Bible class, the Pastor or teacher will be available to help you find the answers to questions that you may have difficulty with. Many people have found it helpful to begin their study early in the week so that they have enough time to meditate on the questions that require careful consideration.

Your answers should be written in your own words in the space provided on the weekly studies with appropriate verse references unless the question calls for a personal opinion. The answers to the questions will be found in the Scripture references at the end of the questions or in the passages listed at the beginning of each study.

How to use this study guide.

The Lamplighters discipleship materials are designed for a variety of ministry applications. They have been used successfully in the following settings.

Self-study - Read the passage carefully that is listed at the beginning of the weekly lesson. Seek to gain as much understanding of the Text as possible. Answer the questions in the space provided using complete sentences if the space allows. Complete the entire lesson without looking at the Leader's Guide in the back of the book. Discipline yourself to answer all the questions so that you gain the maximum benefit from the lesson. When you have completed the lesson, read the corresponding portion of the Leader's Guide to gain greater understanding of the passage you have studied.

One-on-one discipleship - Complete the entire lesson without referring to the Leader's Guide. If you are leading the one-on-one discipleship time meeting, become familiar with the Leader's Guide answers before you meet with the person you are discipling. Plan to meet for one hour to discuss the lesson. If you are not leading the study, do not look at the Leader's Guide until you have met with the person who is leading the meeting.

Small Group discipleship - The members of the discipleship group should complete their entire weekly lessons without referring to the Leader's Guide. The Group Leader completes the entire lesson and then become thoroughly familiar with the Leader's Guide answers before leading the group discussion. A comprehensive ministry manual has been prepared for leaders to help them lead small groups effectively and to gain understanding how to implement the Lamplighters discipleship ministry into their church ministries.

Class teaching (Adult Bible Classes or an alternative to Sunday School Classes) The pastor or teacher should complete the entire lesson before class, review the Leader's Guide answers and then prayerfully consider how to present the lesson. The class members should complete their weekly lessons in advance so that they can bring their thoughtful insights and questions to the class discussion. The Teacher's Edition makes an excellent companion to this format and allows the teacher to design individual lessons appropriate in length and knowledge level for the students. Contact Lamplighters or visit our website for more information about these two resources.

"Do you think" Questions

Each weekly study has a few "*do you think*" questions. These questions ask you to make personal applications from the biblical truths you are learning. Make a special effort to answer these questions because they are designed to help you apply God's Word to your life. In the first lesson the *"do you think*" questions are placed in italic print for easy identification. If you are part of a study group, your insightful answers to these questions could be a great source of spiritual encouragement to others.

Personal Questions

Occasionally you will be asked to respond to personal questions that you should do your best to answer. If you are part of a study group, you will not be asked to share any personal information about yourself. However, be sure to answer these questions for your own benefit because they will help you compare your present level of spiritual maturity to the biblical principles presented in the lesson.

A Final Word

Throughout this study the masculine pronouns are often used in the generic sense to avoid awkward sentence construction. When the pronouns "he", "him", "his" are used to refer to the Trinity (God the father, Jesus Christ and the Holy Spirit), they always refer to the masculine gender.

This *Lamplighters* study is presented after many hours of careful preparation. It is our prayer that it will help you *"... grow in grace and knowledge of our Lord and Savior Jesus Christ. To Him be the glory both now and forever. Amen."* (2 Pet. 3:18).

About the author ...

John Stewart was born and raised near Winnipeg, Canada. He was drafted by the Pittsburgh Penguins (NHL) and played professional hockey for eight years. He was born again in 1977 and graduated from seminary in 1988. He served as a pastor for fifteen years. During this time he planted two Bible-believing churches and founded Lamplighters International. He currently serves as Executive Director of the ministry.

Study #1a   **Pride And Prejudice**

> Read - Ju. 11:1-12:15; other references as given.

1. When the sons of Israel were confronted by the Lord, they repented of their wickedness, put away their foreign gods, and served the Lord (Ju. 10:16).

    a. What happened this time when Israel repented (Ju. 10:17)?

    b. Since Israel put away the foreign gods among them and served the Lord, why did God summon the Ammonites and allow the Israelites to face more trouble (Ju. 11:24, 32, 33)?

    c. No doubt some of the Israelites were surprised when their repentance was followed by more trouble. Has there ever been a time in your life when you made an important spiritual decision and anticipated God's blessing but only experienced more trouble?   How could you use this passage (Ju. 10:16, 17) to comfort someone who has experienced tribulation immediately after he repented?

2. Even though Israel had already mustered a volunteer army at Mizpah to fight against the Ammonites (Ju. 10:18), they lacked a strong military leader. Give a brief description of the military leader they chose who eventually became Israel's eighth judge (Ju. 11:1-3; 12:7; Heb. 11:32-35).

3. The son of a harlot (v. 1), Jephthah was driven from his home by his own family. Instead of allowing the prejudices and injustices of others to defeat him, Jephthah appropriated the grace of God and allowed his new surroundings to become God's school of learning. He became a valiant warrior and a godly man (cf. Ju. 11:11, 34, 35). Name at least one negative situation you experienced during your childhood that God eventually used to develop godly character in your life?

4. Jephthah had earned such a reputation as a mighty warrior and leader that the leaders of Gilead sought his military leadership (vv. 5-7).

    a. What did the Gileadites promise Jephthah if he would become their military leader (vv. 8, 9)?

    b. Jephthah seemed to be suspicious of the elders of Gilead. What did Jephthah do to solemnize his agreement with the leaders of Gilead (vv. 10, 11)?

5. Even though Jephthah was a valiant warrior (Ju. 11:1), he showed great wisdom as he attempted to negotiate a peaceful settlement with the Ammonites (vv. 12-27).

    a. How did Jephthah try to resolve the conflict with the Ammonites (vv. 12, 14)?

    b. At first glance, the king of Ammon appears to be a man of diplomatic wisdom (v. 13). What did he demand from Israel (v. 13)?

Pride And Prejudice

6. The Scriptures never promise Christians freedom from conflict in this world (cf. Job 5:7; 14:1; Ecc. 2:23). However, God has promised His guidance, wisdom, and peace during the struggles of life. Take a moment to seriously examine your life. Are you like Jephthah, a man who sincerely wanted peace and did all he could to resolve conflict, or like the king of Ammon, a man who wanted conflict even though he made a token offer of peace?

7. The Ammonites wanted the Israelites to return some land (i.e., the land of Gilead) they believed Israel had wrongfully taken from them when Moses led the people out of Egypt to the edge of the Jordan River (v. 13). Jephthah's second messenger gave the king of Ammon three reasons why the land in question should remain in Israel's possession. What are they (Ju. 11:14-27)?

8. Jephthah communicated with the king of Ammon through two groups of messengers (vv. 12, 14 ff.). Their communication with the king of Ammon reveals two important principles that can help all believers resolve interpersonal conflict. What are these two *principles* (vv. 12, 14-26)?

9. Jephthah was unable to resolve the conflict with the king of Ammon with diplomatic negotiations. What three things did Jephthah's messengers tell the king of Ammon (v. 27)?

"Blessed are the peacemakers, for they shall be called sons of God."
Matthew 5:9

Study #1b   Pride And Prejudice

Read - Ju. 11:1-12:15; other references as given.

10. When the king of the Ammonites disregarded Jephthah's explanation (v. 28), Jephthah went throughout the Transjordan territories of Gilead and Manasseh preparing the people for war (v. 29 ff.). Jephthah's desire to defeat the Ammonites was so intense that it led him to make a special **vow to the Lord** (vv. 30, 31).

   a. What did Jephthah say he would vow to the Lord if He would give them victory over the Ammonites (v. 31)?

   b. The Lord allowed Jephthah and his army to defeat the Ammonites (vv. 32, 33). What happened when Jephthah returned to his house (vv. 34, 35)?

11. It seems almost inconceivable that a godly man like Jephthah would offer his own daughter as a burnt offering to the Lord. What evidence is given in this passage to indicate that Jephthah actually did offer his only daughter as a burnt offering (vv. 31-40)?

12. Many biblical scholars do not believe that Jephthah offered his only daughter on a pagan altar as a human sacrifice. They believe that Jephthah consigned her to perpetual maidenhood (virginity), probably in service in the tabernacle. What specific Scriptural support is given to support this interpretation (vv. 37-39; Lev. 18:21; Deut. 12:31)?

13. Even though Jephthah was deeply troubled about the consequences of his vow, both he and his daughter were committed to the fulfillment of their word (v. 35). What does the NT teach about the making and keeping of vows/oaths (Matt. 5:33-37; Acts 18:18; 1 Thess. 2:5; Ja. 5:12)?

14. Once again the Ephraimites caused trouble for their fellow countrymen (Ju. 12:1-7). On two previous occasions serious conflicts nearly developed as a result of their pride, selfishness and anger (cf. Jos. 16:14-16; Ju. 8:1-3). When the Ephraimites confronted Joshua, he challenged them to prove their greatness and to enlarge their own territory (Jos. 16:14-16). When they verbally attacked Gideon, he used great diplomacy to calm their anger (Ju. 8:1-3). What two things did Jephthah do when the Ephraimites verbally attacked him and threatened to burn down his house (Ju. 12:2-4)?

Pride And Prejudice

15. The civil war between the tribes of Gilead and Ephraim was the first major internal conflict in Israel. It is another evidence of the ever-advancing nature of sin and a graphic illustration of the destruction that often results from man's rebellion against God.

    a. Many innocent people die every year as a result of the selfishness of other people (e.g., abortion, drunken driving, etc.). How many people died as a result of Ephraim's sin (Ju. 12:6)?

    b. The Lord enabled Jephthah and the Gileadites to defeat the Ephraimites. During the battle, the Gileadites gained control of the critical fords of the Jordan River. They set up a unique plan that enabled them to determine if those who wanted to cross the Jordan were fugitive Ephraimites. What was their plan (Ju. 12:5, 6)?

16. There are three minor judges mentioned in the eight verses of Judges 12. Since there is nothing negative mentioned about their administration, these judges were probably faithful in their service to God and their fellow Israelites. Please give the names and the length of the reign of each of these three judges (Ju. 12:8-15).

Psalm 119:105 "Your word is a lamp to my feet and a light to my path."

Study #2a The Double-Minded Deliverer

> Read - Ju. 13:1-16:31; other references as given.

1. **Again the children of Israel did evil in the sight of the Lord** (Ju. 13:1). As they entered the seventh and final cycle of sin recorded in the book of Judges, whom did the Lord use to chasten His people (v. 1)?

2. The Philistines migrated from Greece or Crete and invaded the Canaanite coast about 1200 BC. They attempted to expand their territory eastward into Israel. While Philistia occupied much of Israel's land during this period, their rule over the people was not as severe as some of the previous oppressions (e.g., Canaan, Midian).

    a. Samson was the last of the twelve Israelite judges. Name three things that are unique about his birth (vv. 2-5)?

    b. While most Nazarites (Heb. *nazir,* to separate, to consecrate) took their vows for six months or a year, others kept them for their entire lives. Name three distinguishing characteristics of a man who had taken a Nazarite vow (Nu. 6:2-6)?

3. Before the angel of the Lord appeared to Manoah and his wife (vv. 2-20), this heavenly figure revealed himself to many others (cf. Gen. 22:1-18; 31:11-13; Ex. 3:1-6; Ju. 6:11-24).

    a. For what did Manoah pray when his wife told him about the appearance of the angel of the Lord (v. 8)?

b. Many scholars believe the angel of the Lord in the OT is the pre-incarnate person of Jesus Christ. This is known as a theophany, a visible appearance of God. Give three evidences from Judges 13:11-22 that support this interpretation (cf. Ex. 3:13, 14; Isa. 9:6).

4. There is no mention of Israel's supplication or repentance during the entire judgeship of Samson. Apparently the Israelites had become complacent and had learned to live under the dominion of their oppressors. Like the Israelites, many Christians seem content to live under the oppression of sin (anger, bitterness, lust, jealousy, etc.). Why do you think some believers tolerate sin in their lives when Christ has promised freedom (cf. Jn. 8:32, 36; 1 Cor. 10:13)?

5. Even though the Israelites were content to be under the dominion of the Philistines, the Lord still extended His grace to them.

    a. Please list at least three evidences of God's grace during this time (Ju. 13:3, 5, 25).

    b. There are many parallels between ancient Israel during the times of the judges and modern America. What do you think are some evidences that God's grace and mercy are at work today in America?

The Double-Minded Deliverer

6. Samson (Heb. *sunny* or *brightness*) is a prime example of a carnal believer who is double-minded and unstable in all his ways (cf. Ja. 1:8). Raised by godly parents (Ju. 13:8, 19) and endowed with privileges from God (Ju. 14:19), Samson fraternized with the enemy and failed to fulfill God's plan for his life.

   a. Name at least five reasons why Samson was so ineffective in the Lord's service (Ju. 14:1-3, 6, 7)?

   b. The phrase **his father and mother did not know that it was of the Lord** (Ju. 14:4) seems to contradict God's prohibition against marrying heathen (cf. Deut. 7:1-4). If this phrase is not God's endorsement of Samson's marriage to a heathen, what does it mean (v. 4)?

7. Only Samson and his father went down to Timnah to his wedding and the marriage feast (v. 10 ff.). It is likely that fear of the Philistines was not the main reason why more people did not attend the wedding. Perhaps some were knowledgeable of his noble birth and the Nazarite vow and were opposed to the marriage. Do you think Christians (including family members) should attend the wedding of a believer who is marrying a non-Christian, including family members?   Why?

8. Many scholars believe Samson violated his Nazarite vow when he took the honey out of the carcass of the lion (v. 9; cf. Nu. 6:6). If this is true, what do you observe about Samson's attitude toward sin that is characteristic of all carnal believers (Ju. 14:12-14)?

Study #2b   The Double-Minded Deliverer

> Read - Ju. 13:1-16:31; other references as given.

9. Samson told his Philistine friends a riddle at the wedding feast (Ju. 14:14). The Philistines threatened to kill his wife and burn down her father's house if she did not get Samson to tell her the riddle (v. 15). What three things did she do to get Samson to tell her the riddle (Ju. 14:16, 17)?

10. Samson was a man dominated by his flesh. Lustful and irreverent, Samson lived in a perpetual state of emotional and spiritual turmoil. What other negative characteristics do you observe about his life (Ju. 14:19-15:5)?

11. Samson caused great economic destruction to the Philistines by burning their shocks (sheaves of standing grain ready to be harvested), crops, vineyards, and groves (Ju. 15:5). The Philistines retaliated by killing his former wife and her father (v. 5).

    a. As Samson rationalized his revenge, he made an important statement that is similar to the excuse many people give before they sin. What is this statement (v. 7)?

    b. Do you rationalize wrong behavior by saying you will stop the habit later?

12. The Philistines threatened the Israelites, forcing them to capture and bind Samson, who was delivered into their hands (vv. 9-13). The Spirit of the Lord came upon Samson mightily and God used him to be His instrument of judgment on the Philistines (Ju. 15:14-17). Unlike Israel's other judges, Samson acted alone in his acts of aggression.

a. Take a minute to examine the history of the conflict between Samson and the Philistines (Ju. 14:19-15:16). Besides God's command against vengeance, why do you think Christians should not engage in revengeful conduct?

b. What are some common types of retaliation that Christians use that are condemned as evil (Gal. 5:20; 1 Pet. 3:9)?

13. Samson entered into Philistia again and sought the affections of another Philistine woman (Ju. 16:1 ff.; Gaza was one of the five main Philistine cities). If God hadn't delivered Samson, his lustful conduct would have enabled the Philistines to capture him (v. 3). Unwilling to learn from his errors and blinded by lust, he fell in love with a woman named Delilah, whose close affiliation with the Philistine lords suggests that she was a Philistine (cf. Ju. 16:5).

   a. What three lies did Samson tell Delilah regarding the secret of his strength (vv. 7, 11, 13)?

   b. In Samson's three responses to Delilah, he missed three excellent opportunities to witness to the power of God. Why do some Christians miss many opportunities to testify to the grace of God (Matt. 16:23)?

14. What similarities do you observe between his former wife's attempt to get him to tell her the meaning of the riddle and Delilah's attempt to get Samson to tell the secret of his strength (Ju. 14:16, 17; 16:15, 16)?

15. When Samson told Delilah the secret of his strength, he was betrayed by his own folly. Finally under their control, the Philistines blinded Samson and made him their slave (v. 21). Although blinding the eyes of an enemy was a common military practice, it is interesting that this fate befell Samson (v. 21). The specific loss of his sight teaches an important principle about God's individual judgment in the lives of His people. What do you think this principle is?

16. Because of his unwillingness to obey the Lord, he went from a deliverer of God's people to a slave in the camp of sin. Oh, the price God's people pay for their folly! What are some other negative results when God's people allow themselves to become slaves of sin (Ju. 16:23-25)?

17. God will not be mocked. Even if His people become a laughingstock, He will not allow His name to be despised.

    a. How did God vindicate His holy name when the Philistines were amusing themselves at Samson's expense (vv. 28-30)?

    b. Samson, Israel's double-minded deliverer, is an excellent example of what not to do in the Christian life. List three specific characteristics you have observed in Samson's life.

Study #3a The Fruit Of Self-Deception

Read - Ju. 17:1-18:31; other references as given.

The death of Samson (Ju. 16:30) brings the chronological section of the period of the Judges to an end. Judges 17:1-21:25 is an appendix to the book of Judges that deals with the general spiritual and moral conditions of the Israelites during the early time of the Judges (cf. Ju. 18:1 ff.).

1. An Ephraimite named Micah (Heb. *who is like Jehovah?*) stole eleven hundred pieces of silver from his mother (Ju. 17:2). Fearful of his mother's curse, Micah confessed his sin and returned the money to his mother (v. 3).

    a. What was the *first* thing Micah's mother did when he returned the stolen money (v. 3)?

    b. What did she want Micah to do with the two hundred pieces of silver (v. 3)?

2. The ancient proverb **like mother, like daughter** (Eze. 16:44) and the modern proverbial expression "Like father, like son" teach the same principle - the character traits of one generation are often duplicated in the next. Name at least two negative character traits that are seen in both Micah and his mother (vv. 2-5; cf. Col. 3:5).

3. Often one generation's character strengths and weaknesses are passed down to the next generation without serious consideration of their consequences. Unfortunately, this lack of self-reflection has caused many believers to reap the fruits of their own self-deception and blindness.

The Fruit of Self-Deception

    a.   What negative character traits have you observed in your parents that have been a struggle for you to overcome? (Note: If you answer this question during the Group Discussion Time, be sure to honor your father and mother; cf. Eph. 6:2.)

    b.   Some Christians believe that they are the hopeless victims of the sins of previous generations (cf. Ex. 20:5). What has God provided to rescue man from his natural tendency to repeat the sins of previous generations (2 Cor. 5:17; Jn. 17:17; Ga. 5:16)?

4.   Apparently Micah and his mother saw nothing wrong with dedicating the money to the Lord and then using it to purchase an idol (Ju. 17:3, 4). In the same way, some believers do not see a problem when they worship the Lord on Sunday and then offer themselves and their resources on the pagan altars of this world throughout the week. What did Micah do after the graven image had been completed (vv. 4, 5)?

5.   The statement **In those days there was no king in Israel; everyone did *what was* right in his own eyes** (v. 6) is emphasized throughout the remainder of the book (cf. Ju. 18:1; 19:1; 21:25). The verse serves as a summary assessment of the book of Judges and a solemn warning to all those who reject the authority of God's Word.

    a.   Now that you have learned that the last five chapters of Judges are an appendix to the book rather than part of the continuing chronology, what specific time period do you think is meant by the phrase **In those days** (v. 6)?

The Fruit of Self-Deception 21

b. Look closely at the phrase **... there was no king in Israel** (v. 6). The biblical writer seems to emphasize the fact that the absence of centralized authority (i.e., king) contributed to widespread social relativism and the spiritual corruption in the nation. This verse teaches an important spiritual principle. What is it?

c. Other than the authority of God's Word, what are some things modern man (including Christians) uses as his standard for living?

6. If man does not allow himself to be evaluated by God's Word, how will he naturally assess his own actions (v. 6)?

7. Of the forty-eight cities originally designated as Levitical cities (cf. Jos. 21:1-42), Bethlehem in Judea was not one of them. A Levite, who is later identified as Jonathan (cf. Ju. 18:30), had moved from one of the Levitical cities to Bethlehem before he traveled north to Ephraim in search of a permanent home (Ju. 17:7, 8).

   a. If the Levites were supposed to settle in these specific Levitical cities so they could be available to teach the Mosaic Law to the people, why do you think Jonathan had moved and was now searching for a new home?

   b. Compare the price that Micah and his mother paid for the graven image and the amount of yearly financial support Micah offered to pay Jonathan (vv. 3, 4, 10). If Micah and his family were typical of the spiritual climate of the nation, what do you think this indicates about the spiritual focus of the Israelites?

Study #3b The Fruit Of Self-Deception

Read - Ju. 17:1-18:31; other references as given.

8. Micah and his family set up a shrine in the home (v. 5). He consecrated one of his own sons to be his priest (v. 5) and later "upgraded" when he was able to secure the services of a Levitical priest (vv. 10, 11). Yet he boldly stated that he expected the Lord (i.e., Jehovah) to prosper or bless him (v. 13).

    a. What words do you think could be used to describe Micah's form of worship (vv. 5, 10-13)?

    b. What similarities do you notice between Micah's concept of worship and some of the characteristics of modern religiosity?

9. When the Israelites originally conquered the land of Canaan, the individual tribal allotments were chosen by lot (Jos. 14:1-5; note: the lot was a small device used to determine God's will and to squelch strife; cf. Pro. 16:33; 18:18). Although the tribe of Dan had received a choice territory (cf. Jos. 19:40-48) and the promise of God's victory over all remaining resistance (cf. Jos. 23:1-5), many of the Danites were not content with their inheritance. They sought a new homeland far away from their enemies, the Philistines and the Amorites. Take a minute to assess the Danites' decision to move from their original tribal allotment to the security of another area. Do you think their decision to move was wise or the result of a lack of faith? Why?

10. Like Moses and Joshua before them, the Danites sent out spies to find a suitable place to relocate the tribe (Ju. 18:2). When they came to the hill country of Ephraim and the home of Micah, the Danites recognized Jonathan the Levite (v. 3). Sometimes believers seek counsel from the wrong people and become confused about God's will for their lives. What two things should the Danites have recognized about the Levite's life that would prevent him from offering godly counsel to them (vv. 3, 4)?

11. Having received Jonathan's assurance of victory (v. 6), the five spies traveled north and discovered a spacious land where the people dwelt in peaceful security (v. 7). When the spies reported their discovery to the people, the Danites made immediate plans to attack the inhabitants of Laish (v. 9). What did the Danite army of six hundred men do when they came to the house of Micah (Ju. 18:14-18)?

12. The Danites' offer to make Jonathan their priest provides valuable insight into his character and the possible root cause of Israel's spiritual degeneration during the entire period of the Judges. How would you describe Jonathan's actions (vv. 17-20)?

13. What was Micah's reaction when he learned that his religious paraphernalia and his personal priest had been stolen (vv. 22-24)?

14. During his confrontation with the Danites, Micah made several statements that revealed his spiritual emptiness (v. 24). His spiritual plight was similar to all those who place their trust in external religious rituals rather than in the Lord. List at least three things Micah said to the Danites that revealed his spiritual bankruptcy (v. 24).

15. The Danites defeated the inhabitants of Laish and burned the city (v. 27). They rebuilt the city and renamed it Dan (v. 29). They set up the graven image and installed the Levite Jonathan as their priest (v. 30). No doubt many of the Danites believed that the Lord had blessed their decision to move north away from the oppression of the Philistines and the Amorites. However, it is likely that they did not realize that their departure from the southern portion of the land left a void that was quickly filled by the Philistines. The Philistines gained a key stronghold in Israel and continued to trouble the remaining southern tribes for many years.

    a. Now that you have a greater understanding of the consequences of their decision, how would you describe the Danites' decision to leave the tribal allotment God had given them?

    b. The patriarch Jacob's prophecy concerning his son Dan was partially fulfilled when the tribe moved north. How does this ancient prophecy describe the tribe of Dan (Gen. 49:16, 17)?

    c. What spiritual truth(s) did you learn from this passage of Scripture (Ju. 17:1-18:31)?

"Idolatry is man's foolish attempt to dethrone the Living God and enthrone his own superstitious imaginations."

Study #4a   The Depths Of Depravity

> Read - Ju. 19:1-20:48; other references as given.

As the book of Judges draws to a close, the expression of man's wickedness reaches new depths. The last chapters of Judges (chs. 17-21) have been called the darkest corner of the Word of God - a moral abyss that seems unfathomable for the people of God.

1. The phrase **And it came about in those days when there was no king in Israel** (Ju. 19:1) is more than a historical marker that identifies the general period of the Judges. Israel had a king, the Lord God (cf. Ju. 8:23; 1 Sam. 8:6, 7).

    a. Now that you have come this far in your study of the book of Judges, what do you think is specifically meant by the statement *there was* no king in Israel?

    b. As you reflect upon the entire message of Judges, what do you think the repetition of this phrase is emphasizing (17:6; 18:1; 19:1; 21:25)?

2. In the preceding chapters (chs. 17, 18), a Levite named Jonathan left his home and his divine commission to become a spiritual mercenary in Ephraim. In Judges nineteen, another Levite from Ephraim becomes a central figure in one of Scripture's most grisly accounts of moral corruption (Ju. 19:1 ff.).

    a. The unnamed Levite took a concubine from Bethlehem in Judah (v. 1). Some Christians believe that a concubine was similar to a modern day mistress - a woman with whom a married man is having an immoral affair. What evidence is given to prove that the Levite's relationship to his concubine was legitimate (vv. 3, 4)?

    b. The concubine left her husband and returned to her father's home in Bethlehem where she stayed for four months (vv. 1, 2). What was the original cause of the breakup of the marriage (v. 2)?

3. After four months of separation from his wife, the Levite traveled to Bethlehem in an attempt to restore his marriage and bring his wife back to Ephraim (v. 3). The Levite spent four days with his father-in-law, enjoying his generous hospitality (vv. 4-7). On the fifth day the Levite and his wife must have left Bethlehem during mid-to-late afternoon because the daylight was almost gone when they reached Jebus (v. 11, i.e., Jerusalem, which is six miles north). Why didn't the Levite want to spend the night in Jerusalem (v. 12)?

4. The Levite, his wife, and the servant passed by Jebus and traveled three miles north to the Benjaminite city of Gibeah (vv. 13-14). Arriving late, they sat in the open square of the city waiting for an invitation for lodging (v. 15). Give a brief description of the man who finally provided lodging for the weary travelers (vv. 16-24).

5. What happened after they were finally settled in the house (v. 22)?

6. The description of the actual events of their stay in Gibeah reveals the deplorable spiritual and moral condition of the Gibeahites.

    a. There are many similarities between this account (Ju. 19:22-26) and the two angels' visit to Lot's house in Sodom (Gen. 19:2-11). List at least five similarities between the two accounts.

    b. It is likely that the striking similarities between these two accounts is more than coincidental. If this is so, what do you think the parallel between the two events is trying to teach?

7. The old man's offering of his virgin daughter and the concubine to the sexual perverts in Gibeah exposes Israel's low view of women during this period (Ju. 19:24). There is a correlation between the spiritual condition of a particular society and the manner in which they treat their women.

    a. Do you think women in our society are generally treated with the dignity they deserve? Please support your answer.

    b. If a new Christian asked you how he should honor the women God has placed in his life (e.g., his wife, mother, sisters, women at church, etc.), what specific advice would you give him?

8. What did the Levite do to protect himself from the lustful homosexual men of Gibeah (v. 25)?

"It is impossible to sin without offending the holiness of God and adding a measure of blindness to your soul."

Study #4b The Depths Of Depravity

> Read - Ju. 19:1-20:48; other references as given.

9. The Levite thrust his wife out into the night and into the hands of the worthless men of Gibeah. They raped her as he slept comfortably in the house of his host (v. 25). At dawn she returned to their place of lodging and died on the doorstep (vv. 26, 27).

   a. What did the Levite do in the morning when he first saw her (vv. 27, 28)?

   b. What character deficiencies do you notice in the Levite's life that might have caused the original problems in the marriage (vv. 4-6, 25-28)?

10. What did the Levite do when he finally reached his home in Ephraim (v. 29)?

11. The sons of Israel, with the exception of the tribe of Benjamin and the inhabitants of Jabesh-gilead (cf. Ju. 21:5-9), assembled at Mizpah to find out the exact details of the original atrocity (Ju. 20:1 ff.). As the Levite recounted the events of that fateful night in Gibeah, what important detail did he leave out (vv. 4-7; cf. Ju. 19:25)?

12. Before the sons of Israel attacked Gibeah (Ju. 20:8 ff.), they asked the tribe of Benjamin to deliver up the worthless men for execution (vv. 12, 13). According to the Law of Moses, the wickedness had to be removed from Israel to prevent the moral corruption of the entire nation (cf. Deut. 17:11-13).

    a. How did the Benjaminites respond (v. 13)?

    b. The Benjaminites' willingness to defend the Gibeahites was more than an act of tribal loyalty - it revealed a deep spiritual problem within the tribe itself. What was the problem (v. 13)?

    c. What responsibility has God given every local church to prevent the spread of wickedness within the church by those who are not willing to repent (1 Cor. 5:1, 2, 13)?

13. The sin of the worthless Gibeahite men led to the death of the concubine and a civil war between the sons of Israel and the tribe of Benjamin (Ju. 20:14 ff.). During Israel's first attempt to rid the land of the evil influence, they were defeated and twenty-two thousand Israelites were killed (Ju. 20:21). Like the Israelites, Christians are often defeated in their initial attempts to rid themselves of evil habits.

    a. The Israelites did three things that were critical to the ultimate victory over their enemies. What are they (Ju. 20:22, 23)?

b. Take a moment to reflect upon an area of spiritual conflict in your life (e.g., your struggle to stop a sinful habit or your attempt to establish a spiritual habit like reading your Bible, etc.) in which victory has eluded you. How could you apply these three important spiritual principles to your situation?

14. During their second attempt to rid the nation of the evil influence, the Israelites were defeated again (Ju. 20:25). This time eighteen thousand Israelite men died in battle.

    a. With such heavy casualties, why do you think the Israelites continued to fight the Benjaminites?

    b. What important spiritual lesson(s) do you think can be learned from their willingness to continue?

15. The Lord gave the sons of Israel assurance of victory after the second defeat (v. 28). The reference to Phinehas, the son of Aaron, indicates this event took place early in the period of the Judges. Using a military strategy similar to the one used by Joshua at the battle of Ai (cf. Jos. 8:4 ff.), the sons of Israel ambushed the Benjaminites and defeated them (Ju. 20:30-44). What was the total number of casualties that occurred as a result of the Gibeahites' sin (Ju. 19:28; 20:21, 25, 43-48)?

Psalm 119:105 "Your word is a lamp to my feet and a light to my path."

Study #5a   Right In Their Own Eyes

> Read - Ju. 21:1-25; other references as given.

1. The civil war between the Benjaminites and the other eleven Israelite tribes was so fierce that the tribe of Benjamin was almost annihilated. What was the total number of Benjaminites who survived the conflict (Ju. 20:47)?

2. Shortly after the war ended, men from the eleven remaining tribes went to Bethel and lifted up their voices and wept bitterly (Ju. 21:2).

    a. Why did the men weep and cry out before the Lord (Ju. 21:3)?

    b. Do you think the nation suddenly realized that their punishment of the Benjaminites had been too severe or do you think they were genuinely concerned about the tribe's future existence?

3. When the eleven tribes met at Mizpah before the war (cf. Ju. 20:1 ff.), they had taken an oath to not give their daughters in marriage to the tribe of Benjamin (cf. Ju. 21:1, 2). Perhaps the low moral character of the Benjaminites prompted this decision.

    a. Now that there were only a few male survivors, the tribe of Benjamin was facing extinction unless wives were found for the six hundred men. How would you describe the Israelites' attitude toward their former enemies, the Benjaminites, after the civil war (Ju. 21:1-4)?

b. Most people, including Christians, find it difficult to demonstrate biblical love toward those who have recently hurt them. What are some negative ways people respond when they are offended or hurt?

c. Take a moment to examine your own life. Do you quickly reconfirm your love toward those who have hurt you, or do you sometimes hold a grudge or hold yourself aloof from those who need assurance of your love (e.g., family members, friends, fellow believers, people at work, etc.)?

4. The Lord reminded the Israelites that He had brought the people up from Egypt as He had sworn (Ju. 2:1). The Israelites were reminded that the hand of the Lord was against them when they did evil, just as He had sworn (Ju. 2:15). Jephthah swore to offer the first thing that came out of his house to the Lord, and when it was his only child, he said he could not take it back (Ju. 11:31-35). The eleven tribes had sworn that they could not give their daughters to the Benjaminites (Ju. 21:1). They had also sworn to kill those who did not come up to punish the Benjaminites (Ju. 21:5). As you reflect on these various situations involving oaths in the book of Judges, what have you learned about the making and keeping of oaths?

5. When the men of Jabesh-gilead had been originally called to fight against the Benjaminites, they refused to help. Their failure was a violation of the Mosaic Law and regarded as an act of rebellion by the remaining eleven tribes. What did the sons of Israel do when they learned that the men of Jabesh-gilead did not join the fight against the Benjaminites (Ju. 21:10-12)?

Right In Their Own Eyes

6. The word for **breach** (v. 15, Heb. *peres*) is usually associated with an outburst of the Lord's anger (v. cf. 2 Sam. 6:8). Do you think the use of this phrase is stating that the Lord was ultimately responsible for the judgment the Benjaminites received at the hand of their fellow Israelites, or is it evidence that the nation was blaming God for its own failure?

7. All the inhabitants of Jabesh-gilead were killed except four hundred young maidens (Ju. 21:12). These young virgins were given to the Benjaminites as wives so **that a tribe may not be destroyed from Israel** (Ju. 21:17). However, there was still a shortage of two hundred women if every Benjaminite survivor was to have a wife. What plan did the elders of Israel implement to provide wives for the remaining two hundred men (Ju. 21:14-23)?

8. The elders anticipated a negative reaction from the fathers and brothers of the two hundred young maidens who were stolen from the feast at Shiloh. Naturally, they would be upset about the abduction of their family members and concerned about the effects of violating the oath they had sworn at Mizpah (i.e., not giving their daughters to the Benjaminites). What answer did the elders plan to give to the families of the maidens who were abducted (Ju. 21:22)?

"Sin will cost you more than you want to pay, take you farther than you want to go, and give you more misery than you can ever imagine."

Anonymous

Study #5b Right In Their Own Eyes

> Read - Ju. 21:1-25; other references as given.

9. Nothing in this passage seems to indicate that this strange plan for repopulating the tribe of Benjamin met with any resistance from the families of the remaining eleven tribes. If the eleven tribes had been so angry at the Benjaminites that they had sworn to not give their daughters to them in marriage (Ju. 21:18), why do you think they would give up their daughters to the Benjaminites without a conflict?

10. The book of Judges almost closes with an "everyone lived happily ever after" theme (Ju. 21:24). As the Israelite tribes and families returned home after the feast at Shiloh, the tribe of Benjamin had been given a new start and the other eleven tribes must have felt good about their benevolent actions. How do we know that their peace and tranquility were short-lived and that trouble lay ahead (Ju. 21:25)?

11. Why do you think the word **Judges** is an appropriate title for this book?

12. What evidences of the grace of God did you notice throughout your study of Judges?

13. The book of Judges can easily be divided into three major sections. From the summary statements listed below, please match the summary statement that corresponds with the appropriate verse reference:
    1. The chronological section of Judges that details the seven cycles of sin and the ministries of the twelve Israelite judges,
    2. The non-chronological section of Judges that emphasizes that Israel's Spiritual and moral problems were directly related to their failure to acknowledge the Lord God as king,
    3. The historic overview of the book that gives the general reasons why the individual tribes failed to inherit their individual tribal allotments.

    a. Judges 1:1-3:6

    b. Judges 3:7-16:31

    c. Judges 17:1-21:25

14. Like the rest of the Scriptures, the book of Judges was written as an example for our instruction (1 Cor. 10:11).

    a. What important spiritual lessons did you learn from the negative examples you studied in Judges?

b. What important spiritual lessons did you learn from the positive examples you studied in the book?

c. Who in the book of Judges impressed you the most as a person of faith? Please explain your answer.

Congratulations:
You have just completed a challenging study of a difficult portion of God's Word. If you have completed all the studies, you have spent several hours analyzing the consequences of compromise and the tremendous price man pays for sin. Judges' graphic portrayal of sin and its effects was meant to teach you to abhor what is evil. The ministry of the twelve judges was presented to help you realize your need for an authority beyond yourself. In a world that seems passionately preoccupied with a desire to do what is right in its own eyes, may your life point others to the Great Deliverer, Jesus Christ, who alone can rescue man from the perils of this life and eternal judgment.

#1 Pride and Prejudice

1. a. The Lord motivated the Ammonites to attack Israel.

   b. The Lord summoned the Ammonites so that He could use Israel to be His instrument of judgment against the Ammonites (Ju. 11:32, 32). The Ammonites were idolaters who worshipped the pagan god Chemosh (Ju. 11:24).

   c. Answers will vary. This passage is an excellent example of the wisdom and sovereignty of God. As soon as the Israelites repented, the Lord sought to use them for His glory and to show them the majesty of His power. It is very possible that the Israelites thought that the Lord was summoning the Ammonites to chasten them for turning away from the Lord when He had already begun to use them in His service. In the same way, God will use a believer as soon as he truly repents of his sin.

2. Jephthah was the son of a man named Gilead who was from the tribe of Gilead (Ju. 11:1). His mother was a harlot, which probably indicates that she was a Canaanite, since prostitution was almost unknown among the ancient Israelites at this time. He experienced rejection from his half brothers, who drove him from his family and home (v. 2). He settled in the land of Tob (Ju. 11:3), where he became a valiant warrior. He eventually became Israel's eighth judge (Ju. 11:1; 12:7). His inclusion in the "hall of faith" in Hebrews chapter eleven is evidence of his godly character and sincere faith in God.

3. Answers will vary.

4. a. They promised him the leadership of the tribe of Gilead if he led them in a successful military campaign over the Ammonites.

   b. He called on God to witness the commitment he and the elders of the tribe of Gilead had made.

5. a. He sent two groups of messengers who met with the king of Ammon and attempted to resolve the problem. The first group was sent to simply determine the nature of the offense (v. 12) and the second group was sent to explain Israel's perspective (v. 14 ff.).

b. The king of Ammon wanted Israel to return a portion of land to the Ammonites. The king of Ammon believed this land was originally taken by Moses and the children of Israel during their journey to Canaan. The disputed land lay between the Arnon and Jabbok rivers in the land of Gilead (v. 13).

6. Answers will vary.

7.
1. The land in question never belonged to the Ammonites. The land of Gilead was taken from the Amorites, not the Ammonites (v. 15).
2. Sihon, king of the Amorites, had originally attacked Moses and the Israelites when they attempted to enter the land. Israel defended herself and defeated the Amorites, giving them legitimate claim to the land (vv. 16-22).
3. The land had remained in the possession of the Israelites for three hundred years without anyone questioning their occupation of the land (v. 26).

8.
1. At a time of conflict, ask the other party to explain the grievance as completely as possible (v. 12). As they explain their problem, listen carefully and offer no immediate justification. It is important to take some time to digest the allegation(s).
2. In a calm and rational way, explain your understanding of the situation, giving logical support for your perspective.

9.
1. Israel had not sinned against the Ammonites (i.e., their accusation was unjustified).
2. Ammon was wrong to instigate war with the Israelites.
3. The Lord, who is the Judge, would ultimately judge the situation in righteousness. It is likely that Jephthah is saying that the Lord would fight for the Israelites and against the Ammonites if they decided to attack the Israelites. Note: This is the only time in the book of Judges where the Lord is called by this name (i.e., Judge).

10.
a. Jephthah said that whatever came out of his house when he returned in peace after his battle with the Ammonites would be presented to the Lord as a burnt offering.
b. Jephthah's daughter came out to meet him with tambourines and with dancing.

_____ Leader's Guide _____ 39

11. 1. The normal understanding of the phrase "burnt offering" would be a sacrifice (v. 31).
    2. The extreme emotional response of Jephthah when he saw his daughter come out to meet him (v. 35).
    3. The daughters of Israel were up every year to commemorate the daughter of Jephthah (v. 40). Other support for this interpretation includes:
        a. The Hebrew word for sacrifice (olah) in its normal usage indicates a sacrificial offering.
        b. Jephthah was the son of a prostitute and could have assimilated heathen beliefs into his life. Jephthah made a thoughtless vow and felt compelled to fulfill his vow so he would not be embarrassed before others and lose his opportunity for leadership.

12. 1. Jephthah's daughter went with her friends to weep on the mountains because of her virginity (vv. 37, 38). It seems unusual that if she was going to be sacrificed as a human offering she would spend the last two months of her life preoccupied with this one concern.
    2. The Text seems to make a point of the fact that, after she returned from her two-month period of mourning, she had no relations with a man (v. 39). Other answers could include:
        a. In Israel, a burnt offering was not thought of in terms of human sacrifice.
        b. Even though Jephthah had at one time a Canaanite influence, human sacrifice was not prevalent among the Canaanites at this time.
        c. Regardless of Jephthah's background, he was a godly man who is specifically recognized for his faith in God.
        d. As a God-fearing man, he would be aware of the Mosaic prohibition against all human sacrifices.
    Conclusion: Bible scholars are divided on the correct interpretation of Jephthah's sacrifice. However, after careful consideration of all the arguments for both sides, the better interpretation seems to favor Jephthah offering his daughter as a servant in the tabernacle.

13. The NT believer should not make any oaths regarding the future (Matt. 5:33-37; Acts. 18:18; Ja. 5:12). The Christian should say what he means and mean what he says. This does not mean that the believer cannot call God as his witness for past events. On at least a few occasions, the apostle Paul called upon God to witness something that happened in the past (1 Thess. 2:5). This latter point should be a comfort to believers who are asked to testify in court and are asked to swear to tell the truth. In America, people who are conscientiously opposed to giving any kind of oath

have the right to not "swear to tell the truth".

14. 1. Jephthah told the Ephraimites that he had asked for their help but they had refused (vv. 2, 3).
    2. He then gathered the men of Gilead and fought against the Ephraimites and defeated them. Note: It is interesting that the Gileadites seem to have been incited by the Ephraimites' statement that they were fugitives or renegades. Perhaps this accusation offers some insight on how at least the Ephraimites looked at the original settlement of the Gileadites east of the Jordan River.

15. a. Forty-two thousand Ephraimites. While there is no mention of the number of casualties on the other side (Gilead), it is not necessary to assume that there weren't any Gilead casualties during the battle. Even though the Lord could have easily protected the Gileadites, it is more likely that the record of the Ephraimite casualties is included to show the devastating effects of their sinful behavior.
    b. The Gileadites lived on the east side of the Jordan River and controlled the fords on the river. Those people interested in crossing the river had to submit to a test. The test was simple: anyone who wanted to cross had to say the word "Shibboleth" which means "an ear of grain" or "a flowing stream". If they pronounced the word correctly, they were allowed to cross the river without further detainment. If they mispronounced the word by saying "Sibboleth", the Gileadites assumed that they were Ephraimites who were trying to escape back to their homeland. Note: During World War II, the Nazis used a similar plan to identify Russian Jews by requiring them to pronounce the word for corn "kookoorooza".

16. 1. Ibzan the Bethlehemite judged Israel for seven years (vv. 8-10).
    2. Elon the Zebulunite judged Israel for ten years (vv. 11, 12).
    3. Abdon the Pirathonite (probably an Ephraimite, cf. v. 15) judged Israel for eight years (vv. 13-15).

#2 The Double-Minded Deliverer

1. The Philistines.

2. a. 1. His mother was barren before the angel of the Lord visited her.
      2. His birth was divinely announced.
      3. His life's work was decided before he was born.
   b. 1. He was to abstain from wine and strong drink (vv. 3, 4).
      2. He was not to have his hair cut (v. 5).
      3. He was not to touch a dead body (v. 6).

3. a. Manoah prayed that the man of God would return so that he (i.e., the man of God) might teach Manoah and his wife how to raise Samson.
   b. 1. When the angel of the Lord was asked by Manoah if he was the same person who had previously spoken to his wife, the man answered "I am". This specific phrase is known as the "tetragrammaton"; a phrase that is used exclusively in Scripture to identify Jehovah. God told Moses to say that the "I am" had sent him to deliver the children of Israel from Pharaoh (Ex. 3:13).
      2. When Manoah asked the angel of the Lord his name, the heavenly visitor said it was "wonderful" (incomprehensible). This similar designation is used in Isaiah 9:6 to identify the coming Messiah.
      3. Manoah believed that the angel of the Lord was God (vv. 21,22).

4. Like the Israelites, they become complacent and are more willing to live in a state of bondage than fight for their freedom. Man has a tremendous ability to adapt to his surroundings and to tolerate the presence of sin in his life.

5. a. 1. Even though there is no sign of repentance by the Israelites, God visited them and announced the birth of another deliverer.
      2. In the midst of Israel's spiritual bankruptcy, the Lord had providentially raised up two godly people, Manoah and his wife, to raise the deliverer Samson in the fear of the Lord (cf. v. 8).
      3. When Samson grew up, the Lord began to stir him to deliver his people (v. 25).
      4. God tolerated Samson's sinful ways and His willingness to endure the complacency of the Israelites.
   b. 1. Preservation of the nation in spite of national sins that are an abomination to God (e.g., abortion, etc.).
      2. The continued salvation of the lost.

3. Increased interest and effort in the area of church planting and other church ministries.
4. A growing interest in the personal study of the Scriptures. Other answers could apply.

6. a. 1. He was not alert to spiritual danger (v. 1). He demonstrated a severe lack of discernment by frequenting the land of the Philistines. His constant association with evil parallels the testimony of the fool in Proverbs (chs. 5-7) who became entrapped by a harlot (cf. Pro. 7:6-23).
   2. He focused on his own physical satisfaction rather than spiritual fulfillment (vv. 2, 3).
   3. He disregarded the wise counsel of his parents (v. 3).
   4. He lightly esteemed the Word of God (v. 3).
   5. He was not willing to be accountable to others, even his parents (v. 6).
   b. God had raised up Samson to begin to deliver Israel from the hands of the Philistines (Ju. 13:5). It was God's plan to use Samson for this purpose. However, it was Samson's choice (unfortunate as it was) to live out his life as a carnal believer. The Lord will use the carnal efforts of a man like Samson to bring glory to His name. This does not make God the author of sin nor does it mean that He endorses man's sinful conduct in any way. God will use all things to bring glory to Himself, even the wicked, in the day of judgment.

7. Answers will vary. This is a difficult question that must be given much prayer and careful consideration. If a Christian is caught in a dilemma like this (e.g., not wanting to endorse a marriage of a believing friend or family member to a non-believer by attending the wedding but also not wanting to alienate family and friends), he should pray for wisdom and seek godly counsel. Perhaps he could go in private to the believer who is planning to marry a non-Christian and explain why the marriage would be a violation of the Word of God. If the believer plans to continue with his plans to marry against the will of God, the believer should inform the other believer that he/she cannot endorse the marriage in any way. If the Christian believes it would be wise to attend the wedding, the believer who is about to marry a non-believer should be informed that the Christian's presence at the wedding ceremony should not be understood as an endorsement of the marriage. If the believer believes he should not attend the wedding, he should explain in a gracious manner the biblical reasons why he cannot attend. If this position is stated in a firm but

Leader's Guide 43

loving manner and fervent prayer is offered up for the sinning believer, it is possible that the believer may become convicted and cancel the wedding.

8. Samson was not only casual about his obedience to God but he even joked about his sin to others.

9.
   1. She wept (vv. 16, 17).
   2. She made the telling of the riddle a test of Samson's love for her. Married couples would be wise to avoid this manipulative tool.
   3. She nagged him relentlessly (pressed him hard, v. 17).

10.
    1. He had an uncontrolled spirit (Ju. 14:19). He was angry because his wife and thirty friends had tricked him, so he killed thirty people.
    2. He did not resolve problems in his life biblically (Ju. 15:1). When his wife deceived him, he stormed off in anger leaving a major problem in his marriage unresolved. He left his wife for a while, and when he came back, his main focus was not on resolving the past conflict but on winning the physical affections of his wife.
    3. He was vindictive and destructive (Ju. 15:3-5). He lived with unresolved guilt over his previous actions (this time I will be blameless) but still continued to act in a carnal manner.

11.
    a. "But, after that, I will cease."
    b. Answers will vary.

12.
    a. There will be no end to the conflict. Both parties will be led to believe that a final act of retaliation is necessary to even the score. A vengeful spirit will destroy Christians, ruin their witness for Christ and rob them of spiritual joy.
    b. Hatred, contentions, jealousies, outbursts of wrath, dissensions, heresies (factions, Gal. 5:20, 21), reviling, deceit (1 Pet. 3:9). While some of these manifestations of the flesh could simply be expressions of carnal behavior, they could also be used as retaliatory attacks on others.

13.
    a.
       1. He told her if she bound him with seven fresh cords that had not been dried he would become weak (v. 7).
       2. He told her if she bound him with new ropes that had not been used he would become weak (v. 11).
       3. He told her if she wove the seven locks of his hair with the web and fastened it with a pin he would become weak (v. 13).
    b. Their minds are focused on earthly things and they do not see the opportunities

14. 1. Both women made Samson's willingness to tell privileged information a test of "love" (Ju. 14:16; 16:15).
    2. Both women put a tremendous amount of pressure on Samson every day until he gave in (Ju. 14:16; 16:17).

15. Believers will often (but not always) experience God's chastisement in the specific area of their lives in which they have violated His Word.

16. 1. God's enemies become more convinced that their ways are right (v. 23).
    2. God's enemies mock His people (v. 24).
    3. The things of God are not taken seriously (v. 25).
    4. God's enemies look at His people as a source of amusement and entertainment (v. 25).

17. a. He called upon the Lord to give him strength so that he might be avenged of the loss of his two eyes. God gave him strength and Samson pulled on the main support pillars of the building. The pillars gave way and the building collapsed, killing Samson and three thousand Philistines at one time (vv. 28-30). Notice that, even in death, Samson was still preoccupied with his own personal vengeance rather than glorifying the Lord (v. 28).
    b. Answers will vary.

#3 The Fruit of Self-Deception

1. a. She dedicated the entire eleven hundred pieces of silver to the Lord.
   b. She wanted Micah to make a graven image and a molten image. She gave two hundred pieces of silver to a silversmith who made an idol - or idols. It is uncertain if one or two idols were made (cf. Ju. 18:30; note: the Hebrew text indicates one idol was made). Perhaps the graven image and the molten image refer to different parts of the same idol.

2. 1. They are both idolaters (Ju. 17:3, 5).
   2. They are both covetous. Micah stole the money from his mother and his mother dedicated the eleven hundred pieces of silver to the Lord but used two hundred pieces for ungodly purposes.
   3. They are both deceitful. Micah only returned the money he had stolen from his mother under the threat of her curse and his mother feigned dedication of the money to the Lord. Other answers could apply.

Leader's Guide   45

3. a. Answers will vary.
   b. 1. Salvation with its new beginning and its new potential for the future (2 Cor. 5:17).
      2. The Word of God to teach us the truth (Jn. 17:17).
      3. The Holy Spirit who gives believers the strength to live victoriously over sin (Ga. 5:16).

4. When the idol had been completed, Micah set up the idol in his residence. This made his home a local shrine or a miniature temple where local residents could come. He added household idols, secured an ephod, and consecrated one of his sons as a priest. All of these religious actions were totally contrary to the will of God.

5. a. The general period of the Israelite judges.
   b. Man has an essential need for an external authority by which his motives and actions can be evaluated objectively.
   c. Social standards, Hollywood, conscience, reason, religious standards or denominational teachings and the writings of men. Other answers could apply.

6. All his ways seem right in his own eyes.

7. a. 1. Perhaps the Israelites did not give their tithes for the support of the Levitical priests. This would force Jonathan and other Levites to leave their cities in search of financial means of support.
      2. Perhaps Jonathan was discontent with the ministry the Lord had given him or the financial support that was provided to him. Other answers could apply.
   b. If Micah and his mother are typical of the spiritual climate of the nation, the Israelites had forsaken their devotion to the Lord and enthusiastically embraced the pagan practices of the Canaanites. While they continued to manifest an external allegiance to the Lord, their hearts were far from the Lord. They had developed a syncretistic form of religious devotion that was detestable in the eyes of God.

8. a. Answers should include words such as external, formal, ritual and pagan. Other answers could apply.
   b. There appears to be a growing toleration within church ministries of things that are contrary to the Word of God (e.g., psychology, etc.). There is an understanding among many believers that they expect God to bless their lives even though there are things in their lives that are directly contrary to His Word. Other answers could apply.

9. A lack of faith. The Danites had been given their tribal allotment by divine decree and they should have been satisfied with God's provision. Their move caused a vacuum in the land that the Philistines quickly filled. God's people have been called to fulfill God's will and not seek their own selfish pleasure.

10. 1. He was not in the place where he should have been.
    2. He was not doing what he should have been doing. It is never wise for a Christian to seek counsel of a believer who is not walking according to the will of God.

11. The Danite army asked the welfare of the Levite. Next, the five original spies went into Micah's house and stole the graven image and the molten image, the ephod, and the household idols from the house while the six hundred soldiers stood guard at the entrance of the gate (vv. 17, 18).

12. Mercenary. At first Jonathan was upset when the five spies took the idolatrous paraphernalia but was joyous when the Danites offered to make him a father and a priest of the entire tribe of Dan (vv. 18-20). Jonathan's actions are typical of religious opportunists.

13. Micah was upset and gathered some men from the area (probably other idolaters who wanted the shrine to remain at Micah's home) and pursued the Danites. When Micah caught up with the Danites, he confronted them with their theft.

14. 1. "You have taken away my gods …".
    2. "You have taken away "… my priest".
    3. "What do I have besides?" The implied answer to this question is "Nothing." At least Micah had the spiritual sense to realize that the total worth of his religious devotion was bound up in a few pieces of wood and silver and a worthless man who was outside the will of God.

15. a. The Danites were spiritual opportunists who sought personal advantage and their own personal comfort ahead of the will of God.
    b. "A serpent in the way", "a viper by the path".
    c. 1. God has called us to fulfill His plan instead of our own selfish desires.
       2. When we fail to fulfill God's specific plan for our lives, others are affected.
       3. When we fail to fulfill God's plan for our lives, the enemies of God gain great advantage.
       4. Deceitfulness in one generation will often be revealed in the next generation.
       5. It is easy for people to be deceived into thinking that religious observance is synonymous with devotion to God.

Leader's Guide 47

6. God will not bless those individuals who say they are devoted to Him but worship contrary to His plan. Other answers could apply.

#4 The Depths of Depravity

1. a. The Israelites were not willing to acknowledge the authority of God in their lives.
   b. The repetition of this phrase seems to emphasize that the Israelites' failure to acknowledge God's authority was directly related to their difficulties as a people. Throughout the book of Judges the seven cycles of sin serve to remind the reader of the Israelites' inability to learn from their mistakes. The repetition of the phrase "there was no king in Israel" provides a parallel to the cycles of sin and offers a subtle reason for the Israelites' plight.

2. a. The phrases "her husband" (v. 3) and "his father-in-law" (v. 4) prove that their relationship was that of husband and wife. Although a concubine was a legal wife, she held a secondary position in the family.
   b. The concubine had committed immorality against her husband.

3. The city of Jebus was not an Israelite city and perhaps the Levite believed that the city would not be a safe place to lodge.

4. He was an old man from the hill country of Ephraim who had at least one daughter (vv. 16, 24). He had taken up residence in Gibeah and was working in the fields, which possibly identifies him as a farmer (v. 16). He demonstrated the qualities of hospitality and generosity when he invited the Levite and his company to lodge with him for the night and insisted on providing for their needs (v. 20). He was loyal to his guests but he allowed the social standards of his culture to interfere with his obedience to the Lord. He should not have offered his daughter to the wicked men (v. 24).

5. Several homosexual men who lived in Gibeah came to the old man's home and demanded that he deliver the Levite over to them so that they might sexually assault him.

6. a. 1. Both Lot and the old man from Ephraim were living in wicked cities.
      2. Both Lot and the old man insisted on providing hospitality for their guests.
      3. Both Lot and the old man were confronted with the demand to hand over their guest(s) so that the men could commit homosexual acts with them.

4. Both Lot and the old man had been able to raise daughters who were sexually pure in a perverse society.
5. Both Lot and the old man offered their virgin daughters to the sexual perverts who had come to their doors.
6. Both Sodom and Gibeah had reached the point of accepting homosexual behavior within their communities. Additional note: Both cities experienced the judgment of God for their willingness to tolerate sin of this magnitude.
   b. It is possible that the strong parallels between these two accounts teaches that when God's people reject the truth, they will inevitably reach the same depths of depravity as those (e.g., the Sodomites) who are symbolic of man's greatest expression of wickedness.

7. a. Generally not. Within any society that is in the process of breaking away from the truth, there will be signs indicating that women are not being honored according to the biblical standard. Some of the indications that this is happening in America include:
   1. An increase in the sexual exploitation of women (e.g., TV, videos).
   2. The general acceptance of perverse language, including sexual jokes, profanity and "double-meaning statements" in the presence of women.
   3. The expectation of society that women should not be restricted from doing certain physical jobs that men have normally done (e.g., military services, police work, etc.). Other answers could apply.
   b. 1. He should be commended for his spiritual sensitivity and for realizing that God wants him to honor the women in his life.
   2. He should begin to rejoice in God's wonderful design of the woman and accept her uniqueness as a part of God's infinite plan.
   3. He should seek to be understanding as he relates to women and be willing to meet their needs as much as possible.
   4. He should realize that the strengths that God has given him are not to be used to bully or abuse women but to provide strength and emotional support for God's "weaker vessels" (cf. 1 Pet. 3:7). Other answers could apply.

8. The Levite seized his wife and handed her over to them. The use of the word "took" indicates that she was aware of the dilemma and resisted her husband's attempt to make her the object of their wickedness.

9. a. After he arose, he opened the door to find his wife lying on the doorstep. Not realizing she was dead, he told her to get up and get prepared to travel. When she did not respond he realized she was dead. He then placed her dead body on the donkey and traveled north to his home in Ephraim. There is no indication in the Text of remorse or repentance for his sin.

b. He appears totally insensitive to the needs of his wife. Although his four-month delay to restore his marriage could have been due to emotional pain resulting from her adultery, his actions at the home of his father-in-law seem to support this assessment of his character. The Text indicates that he spent the time "fellowshipping" with his father-in-law rather than restoring the broken relationship with his wife. His actions at Gibeah were deplorable. He not only chose to sacrifice his wife to the sexual perverts of the city but his actions the next morning indicate more than those of an emotionally wounded individual.

10. He took a knife and laid hold of his concubine and cut her in twelve pieces, limb by limb, and sent the pieces to the twelve tribes of Israel, including the offending tribe of Benjamin.

11. The Levite left out the fact that he had delivered his own wife over to the worthless men of Gibeah. This is a good example of how easy it is to recount the errors of others but overlook the faults that reveal our own sins.

12. a. The sons of Benjamin would not listen to the voice of the rest of Israel.
    b. The Benjaminites were more willing to demonstrate tribal loyalty than loyalty to the truth. While God's people need to be devoted to one another (cf. Ro. 12:10), they should never allow their loyalty to others to cause them to be disloyal to God and His Word.
    c. God has given every local church the responsibility of separating from those who claim the name of Christ but continue to live in willful rebellion against God. This separation includes all those who profess to be believers even though their lives give little or no indication of true conversion to Jesus Christ (cf. 1 Cor. 5:11 "so-called believer"). It is important to remember that the purpose of separating from certain believers is to help them understand their need for repentance and to protect other believers in the church from a complacent attitude toward sin.

13. a. 1. They encouraged themselves (v. 22). 2. They prepared immediately for battle (v. 22). 3. They inquired of the Lord (v. 23).
    b. 1. When a believer suffers spiritual defeat, he should encourage himself and others by realizing that he is engaged in an intense spiritual battle. He should not allow the defeats of life to destroy him but he should allow them to draw him closer to God.
       2. He should get prepared for more spiritual conflict (including the realization of the present spiritual battle he finds himself in; i.e., the conflict in his mind to give up). To do this he should continue to do the things that he knows are right, such as reading the Word, fellowshipping with other believers and obeying God's commands.
       3. He should seek the Lord in prayer, asking Him to reveal sin in his life and asking for Divine guidance.

14. a. They were commanded by God (through the Law) to rid the nation of the evil influence. In some respects, the casualties were irrelevant because the nation could expect even greater losses as a result of God's coming judgment if they did not deal with this direct violation of God's Word.
    b. Christians must be willing to battle against the forces of evil even though the casualty rate might be high. There must be simply no compromise with evil. If evil activity is allowed to go unchecked in a particular society it will continue to exploit the innocent, paralyze the fearful, prey on the naive, and destroy the very fabric of society.

15. The Levite's wife, forty thousand men from Israel, twenty-five Benjaminites and all the people whom they found in Gibeah when they destroyed the city. Total: sixty-five thousand and one, plus an undetermined number of others. What a price man pays for sin!

#5   Right In Their Own Eyes

1. Six hundred.

2. a. The remaining Israelite tribes were concerned that the tribe of Benjamin would become extinct.
   b. The sons of Israel were genuinely concerned about the Benjaminites' future. The Text does not mention the Israelites experiencing any remorse or guilt over their near annihilation of the Benjaminites.

3. a. The Israelites were genuinely concerned for their brothers. Their response is a good example of how Christians should respond after they have experienced interpersonal conflict with others. The Israelites confronted the problem directly, conquered the problem courageously, and reaffirmed their love quickly toward their enemies, the Benjaminites.
   b. Resentment, anger, frustration, gossip, malice, slander, avoidance and bitterness. Other answers could apply.
   c. Answers will vary.

4. 1. Christians should not make oaths or swear about the fulfillment of future events over which they have no control.
   2. A believer should realize that an oath should be taken seriously. The Christian should do his best to fulfill the oath even if changing circumstances make it difficult to fulfill. Other answers could apply.

5. They sent twelve thousand valiant soldiers to attack the city of Jabesh-gilead. The soldiers killed everyone in Jabesh-gilead except four hundred young virgins. After the battle, the Israelite soldiers brought the four hundred young maidens back to their camp at Shiloh.

6. The Lord was ultimately responsible for the demise of the Benjaminites. He used the eleven remaining Israelite tribes to be His instrument of judgment for the Benjaminites' unwillingness to deal with the sin within the tribe. Note: God often uses secondary causation to judge the world and accomplish His purposes.

7. The elders of Israel told the two hundred remaining Benjaminite men who had not received wives to go up to Shiloh during the annual feast (probably the feast of Tabernacles) and hide in the vineyards (vv. 19, 20). When the young maidens came out to dance, the Benjaminites were to each capture a maiden and return to the land of Benjamin (v. 21).

8. The elders planned to say that the young ladies were taken by the men of Benjamin rather than given by the men of Israel. This released the Israelite men, who had lost their daughters from their previous oath they had taken, to not give their daughters to the Benjaminites. If the fathers of the young women who were taken reacted negatively to the plan, the elders planned to encourage the fathers to give their daughters voluntarily to meet the needs of the Benjaminites.

9.
   1. Even though the tribes were grieved and angry over the sin of the men of Gibeah, there was a national patriotism or solidarity among the Israelite tribes that motivated them to help their brothers.
   2. The plan absolved them of responsibility to the oath and met the need of their Israelite brothers, enabling the Benjaminites to rebuild their tribe. The tribe was so successfully restored that it was able to produce Israel's first king, Saul.

10. The book of Judges closes with the statement that every man did what was right in his own eyes.

11. While the book of Judges offers a detailed presentation of the seven cycles of sin during the three hundred and fifty years from the death of Joshua to the beginning of the monarchy, the real focus of the book is on the ministry of judges or deliverers that God sent to rescue His people from the oppression of their enemies. Imperfect as the judges were, God used these men and women as His agents to deliver the Israelites and demonstrate His grace to the people.

12.
   1. God's willingness to endure the sinfulness of the Israelites in spite of their continuing lack of repentance.
   2. The provision of the twelve Israelite judges who were used by God to deliver the Israelites from their oppressors.

3. God's miraculous working on behalf of the Israelites to rescue His people (the peasant Shamgar killing six hundred Philistines [cf. 3:31], the torrents of rain that helped Deborah and Barak [cf. Ju. 5:21], the fear in the hearts of the Midianites (cf. Ju. 7:13, 14), etc.).
4. God's willingness to patiently endure the lack of faith of those He called to judge Israel (Gideon, Samson). Other answers could apply.

13. a. Judges 1:1-3:6 - the historic overview of the Book that gives the general reasons why the individual tribes failed to inherit their individual tribal allotments.
    b. Judges 3:7-16:31 - the chronological section of Judges those details the seven cycles of sin and the ministries of the twelve Israelite judges.
    c. Judges 17:1-21:25 - the non-chronological section of Judges that emphasizes that Israel's spiritual and moral problems were directly related to their failure to acknowledge the Lord God as king.

14. a. Answers will vary.
    b. Answers will vary.
    c. Answers will vary.

For additional Lamplighters discipleship materials, contact your local Christian bookstore or visit our website at www.LamplightersUSA.org.

The Final Exam

Every person will eventually stand before God in judgment – the final exam. The Bible says, *"And it is appointed for men to die once, but after this comes judgment"* (Heb. 9:27).

May I ask you a question? *"If you died today, do you know for certain that you would go to heaven?"* I did not ask you if you are religious or if you are a church member; nor did I ask you if you have had some encounter with God - a meaningful, spiritual experience. I did not even ask you if you believe in God, angels, or if you are trying to live a good life. The question I am asking you is this: *"If you died today, do you know for certain that you would go to heaven?"*

When you die, you will stand alone before God in judgment. You will either be saved for all eternity or you will be separated from God for all eternity in what the Bible calls the lake of fire (Ro. 14:12; Rev. 20:11-15). Tragically, many religious people who believe in God are not going to be accepted by Him when they die.

"Many will say to Me in that day, `Lord, Lord, have we not prophesied in Your name, cast out demons in Your name, and done many wonders in Your name?' And then I will declare to them, `I never knew you. Depart from Me, you who practice lawlessness!'" *(Matt 7:22, 23).*

God loves you and wants you to go to heaven (Jn. 3:16; 2 Pet. 3:9). If you are not sure where you will spend eternity, you are not prepared to meet God. God wants you to know for certain that you will go to heaven.

"Behold, now is the accepted time, behold now is the day of salvation" *(2 Cor. 6:2).*

The words **"behold"** and **"now"** are repeated because God wants you to know that you can be saved today. You do not need to hear those terrible words, *"Depart from Me..."* Isn't that great news?

Jesus Himself said, **"You must be born again"** (Jn. 3:7). These are not the words of a pastor, a church or a particular denomination. They are the words of Jesus Christ Himself. You <u>must</u> be born again (saved from eternal damnation) before you die; otherwise, it will be too late when you die! You can know for certain today that God will accept you into heaven when you die.

"These things I have written to you who believe in the name of the Son of God that you may <u>know</u> that you have eternal life ..." *(1 Jn. 5:13).*

The phrase, *"... you may know"* means that you can know for certain before you die that you will go to heaven. To be born again, you must understand and believe (this means to place your faith in) four essential spiritual truths. These truths are right from the Bible so you know you can trust them – they are not some man-made religious traditions. Now let's consider these four essential spiritual truths.

1st **Essential Spiritual Truth.** <u>The Bible teaches that you are a sinner and separated from God.</u>

No one is righteous in God's eyes, including you. To be righteous means to be totally without any sin, even a single act.

"There is none righteous, no, not one; There is none who understands; There is none who seeks after God. They have all turned aside; They have together become unprofitable. There is none who does good, no, not one." (Ro. 3:10-12).

"for all have sinned and fall short of the glory of God." (Ro. 3:23)

Look at the words God uses to show that all men are sinners – "**none, not one, all turned aside, not one**". God is making a point – all men are sinners, including you. No man is good (perfectly without sin) in His sight. The reason is sin.

Have you ever lied, lusted, hated someone, stolen anything or taken God's name in vain, even once? These are all sins. Only one sin makes you a sinner and unrighteous in God's eyes.

Are you willing to admit to God that you are a sinner? If you are, then tell Him right now you have sinned. You can say the words in your heart or out loud - it doesn't matter, but be honest with God. Now check the box if you have just admitted you are a sinner.

❏   *God, I admit I am a sinner in your eyes.*

Now, let's look at the second essential spiritual truth.

2nd **Essential Spiritual Truth.** <u>The Bible teaches that you cannot save yourself or earn your way to heaven.</u>

Man's sin is a very serious problem in the eyes of God. Your sin separates you from God, both now and for all eternity unless you are born again.

"For the wages of sin is death …" (Romans 6:23).

"And you He made alive, who were dead in trespasses and sins," (Eph. 2:1).

Wages are a payment that is earned by a person for what he or she has done. Your sin has earned you the wages of death which means separation from God. If you die without ever having been born again, you will be separated from God after death.

You cannot save yourself or purchase your entrance into heaven. The Bible says that man is, *"… not redeemed with corruptible things, like gold or silver …"* (1 Pet. 1:18). If you owned all the money in the world, you could not buy your entrance into heaven, nor can you buy your way into heaven with good works.

"For by grace you have been saved through faith and that <u>not of yourselves;</u> it is the gift of God, <u>not of works lest any one should boast.</u>" (Eph. 2:8, 9)

The Bible says salvation is, *"not of yourselves", "... not of works lest any one should boast."* Salvation from eternal judgment cannot be earned by doing good works – it is a gift of God. There is nothing you can do to purchase your way into heaven because you are already unrighteous in God's eyes.

If you understand you cannot save yourself, then tell God right now that you are a sinner, separated from Him and you cannot save yourself. Check the box below if you have just done that.

- ❏ *God, I admit that I am separated from You because of my sin. I realize that I cannot save myself.*

Now let's look at the third essential spiritual truth.

3rd Essential Spiritual Truth. <u>The Bible teaches that Jesus Christ died on the cross to pay the complete penalty for your sin and to purchase a place in heaven for you.</u>

Jesus Christ, the sinless Son of God, lived a perfect life, died on the cross and rose from the dead to pay the penalty for your sin and purchase a place in heaven for you. He died on the cross on your behalf, in your place, as your substitute, so you do not have to go to hell. Jesus Christ is the only acceptable substitute for your sin.

"For He (God, the Father) made Him (Jesus) who knew (committed) no sin to be sin for us, that we might become the righteousness of God in Him" (2 Cor. 5:21).
"I (Jesus) am the way, the truth, and the life. No one comes to the Father except through me." (Jn. 14:6).
"Nor is there salvation in any other, for there is no other name under heaven given among men by which we must be saved." (Acts 4:12).

Jesus Christ is your only hope and means of salvation. Because you are a sinner, you cannot pay for your sins but Jesus paid the penalty for your sins by dying on the cross in your place. Friend, there is salvation in no one else – not angels, not some religious leader, not even your religious good works. No religious act such as baptism, confirmation or joining a church can save you. There is no other way, no other name who can save you. Only Jesus Christ can save you. You must be saved by accepting Jesus Christ's substitutionary sacrifice for your sins or you will be lost forever.

Do you see clearly that Jesus Christ is the only way to God in heaven? If you understand this truth, tell God that you understand and check the box below.

- ❏ *God, I understand that Jesus Christ died to pay the penalty for my sin. I understand that His death on the cross is the only acceptable sacrifice for my sins.*

4ᵗʰ Essential Spiritual Truth. <u>**By faith, you must trust in Jesus Christ alone for eternal life and call upon Him to be your Savior and Lord.**</u>

Many religious people admit they have sinned. They believe Jesus Christ died for the sins of the world but they are not saved. Why? Thousands of moral, religious people have never completely placed their faith in Jesus Christ <u>alone</u> for eternal life. They think they must believe in Jesus Christ as a real person and do good works to earn their way to heaven. They are not trusting Jesus Christ alone. To be saved, you must trust in Jesus Christ <u>alone</u> for eternal life. Look what the Bible teaches about trusting Jesus Christ alone for salvation.

> *"that if you confess with your mouth the Lord Jesus and believe in your heart that God has raised Him from the dead, <u>you will be saved</u>. For with the heart man believes unto righteousness, and with the mouth confession is made unto salvation. For there is no distinction between Jew or Greek, for the same Lord over all <u>is rich to all</u> who call upon Him. For <u>whoever calls on the name of the Lord shall be saved</u>" (Ro. 10:9, 10, 12, 13).*

Do you see what God is saying? To be saved or born again, you need to trust Jesus Christ <u>alone</u> for eternal life. Jesus Christ paid for your complete salvation. Jesus said, *"It is finished"* (Jn. 19:30). Jesus paid for your salvation completely when He shed His blood on the cross for your sin.

If you believe that God resurrected Jesus Christ (proving God's acceptance of Jesus as a worthy sacrifice for man's sin) and you are willing to confess the Lord Jesus Christ as your Savior and Lord (lord, master of your life), you will be saved.

Friend, right now God is offering you the greatest gift in the world. God wants to give you the <u>gift</u> of eternal life, the <u>gift</u> of His complete forgiveness for all your sins, and the <u>gift</u> of His unconditional acceptance into heaven when you die. Will you accept His free gift now, right where you are?

Are you unsure how to receive the gift of eternal life? Let me help you. Do you remember that I said you needed to understand and accept four essential spiritual truths. First, you admitted you are a sinner. Second, you admitted you were separated from God because of your sin and you could not save yourself. Third, you realized that Jesus Christ was the only way to heaven – no other name could save you.

Now, you must call upon the Lord Jesus Christ once and for all to save your lost soul. Ask Him right now to save you. Just take God at His Word – He will not lie to you! This is the kind of simple faith you need to be saved. If you are still uncertain what to do, pray this prayer to God. Remember, the words must come from your heart.

> *God, I am a sinner and deserve to go to hell. Thank you Jesus for dying on the cross for me and for purchasing a place in heaven for me. Please forgive me for all of my sins and take me to heaven when I die. I call on you Jesus right now to save me forever. Thank you for saving me now. Amen.*

Appendix 57

If you just asked Jesus Christ to save you the best you know how, then God just saved you. He said in His Holy Word, *"Whoever calls upon the name of the Lord will be saved"* and the **whoever** includes you - it is that simple. God just gave you the gift of eternal life by faith. You have just been born again according to the Bible.

You will not come into eternal judgment and you will not perish in the lake of fire – you are saved forever! Read this verse over carefully and let it sink into your heart.

"Most assuredly, I say to you, he who hears My word and believes in Him who sent Me has everlasting life, and shall not come into judgment, but has passed from death into life." (Jn. 5:24)

Now let me ask you a couple more questions. According to God's Holy Word (Jn. 5:24), not your feelings, what kind of life did God just give you? _____. What two words did God say at the beginning of the verse to assure you that He is not lying to you? _____ _____. Are you going to come into judgment - YES or NO? Have you passed from spiritual death into life - YES or NO?

Friend, you have just been born again. You just became a child of God. We would like to help you grow in your new Christian life. We will send you a Spiritual Birth Certificate to remind you of your spiritual birthday and some Bible study materials to help you understand more about the Christian life. To receive these helpful materials free of charge, photocopy the form below, fill it out and send it to us by mail or you can e-mail us at <u>resources@LamplightersUSA.org</u>.

Lamplighters Response Card

- ❏ I just accepted Jesus Christ as my Savior and Lord on (date) _____, 200____ at _____.
- ❏ Please send me the Spiritual Birth Certificate and the Bible Study materials to help me grow as a Christian.
- ❏ I would like to begin attending a Bible-believing church in the area where I live. Please recommend some Bible-believing churches in the area where I live.
- ❏ I already know of a good Bible-believing church that I will be attending to help me grow as a new Christian.

Name _____

Address _____

City _____ State _____ Zip _____

Email address _____

Lamplighters International, P.O. Box 44725 Eden Prairie, Minnesota 55344